Are the Humanities Inconsequent?

Are the Humanities Inconsequent?
Interpreting Marx's Riddle of the Dog

Jerome McGann

PRICKLY PARADIGM PRESS
CHICAGO

Prickly Paradigm Press, LLC
5629 South University Avenue
Chicago, Il 60637

www.prickly-paradigm.com

ISBN-13: 978-0-9794057-6-1
LCCN: 2009923955

Printed in the United States of America on acid-free paper.

According to a recent report (undocumented), a certain professor had assigned Flann O'Brien's *At Swim Two Birds* in an advanced graduate seminar. Class discussion revealed that half the class thought the book "simply frivolous." And this despite the fact that O'Brien's fiction gives a detailed presentation of its theory of aestho-autogamy! Has there been a more arresting contribution to critical discourse since Alfred Jarry's discovery of the science of pataphysics?

To that half class I dedicate this little book—a form of worship chosen from a professor's poetic tale.

Table of Contents

The Argument

A spectre is haunting literature today—the spectre of
'patacriticism.* Nowhere is the threat more evident
than in the late Marxian riddle of the dog: "Outside of
a dog, a book is a man's best friend. Inside of a dog, it's
too dark to read." This book, which explains for the
first time what Marx meant, works from two assump-
tions: 1. That the riddle conceals an allegory about
book culture and is addressed to the academic custodians of book culture; and 2. that our explanation is
necessarily implicated in the problem posed by the
riddle of the dog. It therefore remains to be seen—it is
the reader's part to decide—whether the book is a
friend to man or, perhaps like Marx's riddle, too dark to
read.

---

*'patacriticsm: the study of imaginary interpretations through a science of
exceptional cases.

Part I
PSEUDODOXIA ACADEMICA

Inside a Dog

"Are the humanities inconsequent?" The question is purely—in both senses—academic. Cultural practices flourish all about us in popular and high-brow art, music, writing. It is this high-energy life of our present world that forces the question—the eternal return of *vulgaris eloquio* and its forms of expression: *Grand Theft Auto* (Edition 4!), *Crysis*, *The World Ends with You*. Does our scholastic and critical interest in Wordsworth or Keats, etc., have a public function at the present time. Are we purveying antiquities to an eBay world? A goblin market?

The answer to those questions, I believe, should be "yes, that is precisely our case." We handle these antiquities with care—we take them to our heavens— not because of their virtues but because they are our responsibility. It doesn't matter whether or not we think them deserving of this care or who takes an interest in them or why. As scholars we owe them all our attention in any case. Not as one owes a debt but as one makes a commitment, compelled by love and duty, whether the objects seem—to us, to others, to themselves—deserving or not "on the merits." Rizpah's love—not blind to fault or deceived, but consciously chosen exactly because virtue—not least the virtue of such works—is so uncertain.

It's useful to think—to remember—that there's no such thing as a bad poem. Some poems appear better than others, some appear better to others. But in verse nothing bad can happen, nothing bad will be done. To choose to write a poem is to do something foolish, as every wise person knows. In that choice you make a weighty promise to take care with the language that was given to you. That's why writing a poem is a grave act of secular devotion. To choose to write a poem means that you've already professed your faith in the grace of language. And so the gods are indulgent—where men often are not. So in thinking about poetry after the fact, beware. The gods don't take kindly to those who mistreat their favorites. There *is* such a thing as good and bad criticism.

That's why scholarship, even to pedantry, is criticism's monitor.

Queer as it seems in the world of globalized capital, scholarship will go on with its memorial activities, as classical scholars have long since done with works even more unbelievable than the works of Modernity. (*Think* about Achilles and the other Greek heroes. Heroes? Yes, of course, but also monsters.) Something important is gained when we willingly assume a disbelief in Shakespeare and Rousseau, the Bible and the Upanishads, and consciously sympathize with their weakness and alienation. Byron called it an act of "mobility," Keats called it "negative capability." In each case the move is deliberately taken under the sign of what Byron also called a "spoiler's art." It is heresy in a new key—sympathy with the devil, a latter-day form of Socratic self-questioning. It is the unfinished—the unfinishable—business of scholarship.

> "Perhaps that is a good point to start from again. Perhaps that is what I must learn to accept. To start at ground level. With nothing. Not with nothing but. With nothing. No cards, no weapons, no property, no rights, no dignity." "Like a dog." "Yes, like a dog."
> —Coetzee in *Disgrace*

Or, as a twentieth-century latter day romantic famously put the matter: with the "Nothing that is not there and the nothing that is."

In a Word, Enlightenment

an uncritical absorption in our own
selfrepresentations.
—*The Romantic Ideology*, variant text

The greatest magician (Novalis has memorably written) would be the one who would cast over himself
a spell so complete that he would take his own phan-
tasmagorias as autonomous appearances. Would not
this be our case?
—Borges, "Avatars of the Tortoise"

J: In a word, Enlightenment. With experts presumed to
know.

JD: And then to teach!

J: What they presume they know.

JD: A ludicrous presumption, as The Poet says:

> For me, I know nought; nothing I deny,
> Admit, reject, contemn; and what know you,
> Except perhaps that you were born to die?
> And both may after all turn out untrue.
>
> *—Don Juan*

J: Both?

JD: Well now, there's something you really *should* know—that the poet went on to explain his surprising "Both":

> An age may come, Font of Eternity,
> When nothing shall be either old or new.

I call that a delightful thought, wouldn't you? A 'pata-critical thought for a new kind of academy. Committed to Delightenment.

J: As in Demystify?

JD: And as in Delicious. Think *The Poverty of Enlightenment* turning to *Visions of Excess*. And it would be quite rigorous—scientific! A science of exceptions and imaginary solutions.

J: How do you teach *that*?

JD: It's not about teaching, it's about learning. And as far as learning is concerned, a little teaching is a dangerous thing. The Poet was onto something when he said "He most honors my style who learns under it to destroy the teacher" (Whitman).

J: What kind of style is that?

JD: A theatrical style. A play of teaching made up from scenes of learning. There you'd be, like the dreamer in Borges' "The Circular Ruins," with all your eager imaginary pupils. Everybody's part of the dream you're dreaming, including yourself, the scholar at "an inner-standing-point" (Rossetti). You're there—The Poet said this too—to imagine what you know.

J: What you *think* you know.

JD: Right. That's when you begin to pretend to teach. It won't matter whether we're seeing what you think or watching how you think, whether you're a teacher—as the ancients used to say—"by precept or by example." Either way you're part of the lesson being studied, maybe even being learned. Because now you're being critically absorbed in your own selfrepresentations.

J: Then perhaps scholarship will be ready for its voyagings:

> To follow knowledge like a sinking star
> Beyond the utmost bounds of human thought.
> —Tennyson

Beyond the facts we think we know are the conditions that shape our dreams about those facts. Do we know

what they are,—do we know what we think they are?
Do we know why? Have we tried to find out? It is a
science of possibilities, as The Poet said:

> Effort, and expectation, and desire,
> And something ever more about to be.
>
> —Wordsworth

JD: Could The Poet be misspoken? Did he change his
mind, his view, when he later wrote:

> This never truly being,
> This evermore becoming,
> This spinner's wheel onfleeing
> Outside perception's range.
>
> —Hardy

(PRINTER'S DEVIL. That can't be right, "The Poet."
Perhaps JD meant to say "Three Poets." Or is her Poet
something like Cerberus (or God), "Three Gentlemen
in One"?)

Or this:

> For all experience is an arch wherethrough
> Gleams that untravelled world whose margin fades
> For ever and for ever as I move.
>
> —Tennyson

J: "A man's reach should exceed his grasp, / Or what's a
heaven for?" (Browning)

JD: So many possible worlds imagined into being.
Some we don't like, some we do.

J: But to the scholar, all are fascinating. And we know how to study them, we know their genetic codes.

JD: Do we really? Inside them, what can you see?

J: I can see how they work. I can see the double helix of their molecules—the quantum histories of their productions and their receptions. And I can take their measure.

JD: But can you take your own?

An Old Movie

"He most honors my style who learns under it to destroy the teacher" (Whitman). How does a teacher take that thought to heart? Where do we find the honor that will put our authority to shame?

There is one place, we know, a place where all teachers found their vocation. It is the place, as the Poet said, "where all the ladders" to our cultural heavens start (Yeats). But we forget how foul that place can be, especially when our memories are furnished with the rich decorations of the Poet's verse. Yet surely the Bible was right about the human heart, that it is an offense in the sight of the lord: "the imaginations of man's heart are evil continually." We teachers are the custodians of an ambiguous inheritance—at once beautiful and horrible, splendid and truly, deeply shameful.

How much of that reality can we or should we bear or bring to our students? It's a nice question, it gives me nightmares. Here it comes again, rising on my academic night, digitized and dolbyized. The godlike tones of—who *is* that, Matthew Arnold?—fill the heavy air, the hungry clouds of Blake swag on the deep. Across the darkling plain a large billboard is advertising an old movie, *The Canon Wars*. It is the long-running nightmare of the philosopher and the scholar. How many times have I seen it? Many many. Utterly fascinating... *mythic*! "And thus I am absorbed, and this is life" (Byron): the struggle is engaged, I am there again, full of anxiety, the canon warriors are ravaging the territories and their benighted inhabitants. The scene grows more intellectual, alphabets of people race across the white horizonless expanse. Small groups form randomly, huddling together. As Rintrah roars and shakes his fires in the burdend air [Blake, sic], I watch the terrified letters struggling to articulate themselves. Slowly they are succeeding, they rocket like reversed falling stars into that hungry sky—rising constellations lighting up the billboard in an advertisement for themselves:

> And we are here as on a darkling plain,
> Swept by confused alarms of struggle and flight,
> Where ignorant armies clash by night.
>
> —Arnold

Suddenly I am wide awake and I realize I must communicate this vision. More than that, I must explain its meaning. That is what we do—interpret dreams, visions, and imaginative creations.

Academiana

In the last quarter century, it strikes us that the modernist trajectory that celebrated versions of excess has been emphasized. In this version of modernist aesthetics, the heaping up of detail, to shock, disrupt, engage in carnavalesque gesture or suggest the urban confusion faced by the hapless flaneur, is celebrated a disruptive, subversive, or at least a fertile planting-ground for versions of jouissance-laden supplementarity.

* * * *

In this model, the modernist critique of authenticity involves a negative moment of corrective rejection followed by a further different kind of negativity that recognizes the corrective rejection's inevitable eventual lapse into bad faith (or ideological delusion, or inauthenticity).

* * * *

On Yeats's poem, "Fergus and the Druid"
*   The poem evokes, beyond specific refusals and determinate acts of negative rejection or positive acceptance, a disruptive multiplicity, represented by the bag (reducible neither to Pandora's box nor to Aeolus's bag of winds, aspects of classical myth that leave hierarchies of power involving gender and social position in place). The effects of opening the bag can stand for the multiply framing, polyvocal tendencies of modernist literary discourse, whose ambivalences resist being reduced easily to a dominating, essentializing discourse.*

* * * *

Whether or not they're aware of dancing in the modern/postmodern contact zone, all of these papers read modernist authenticity as not merely contingent but dynamic, balancing on the fulcrum of an insistent temporality, negotiating the tension between overlapping models of group identity, creating itself by means of recurrent self-banishment. And in this they remind us of the suggestive, provoking, contested, perpetually unfinished and self-reinventing nature of the seminar process itself.

****

The detail's potential to erupt as a trace of supplementarity has been most studied in work on the multiple valences of the term "fetishism"; the paradox, however, seems to be that to involve fetishism is also to begin to police it....

****

This paper places the "Aporias" reading in the setting of a weekly research group whose research cycle was creating meaning in and out of the work being done and the continuing dialogues with(in) it. One of the paper's segments consists of an (inter)[texture]al performative to be read with an 11-minute video from a 1-hour studio/gallery session edited into approximately seven minutes with four minutes of visual contextual framing entitled, "(Re)searching Sculpted 'Aporia': (Re)learning (Subverted-Knowing) through Praxis.")

****

The silence that surrounds nonheterosexuality feeds heteronormativity in powerful ways.

An ABC of Interdisciplinarity

A: As Moses Hadas used to say: "The only interesting talk is shop talk."

B: All shops are closed shops, more or less. Suffocating. If you're not a professor and you find yourself by circumstance dropped among a bunch of professors at lunch, how interesting do you imagine you'll find their conversation?

C: Well, suppose you came there as an ethnographer. Then the shop talk might seem very interesting indeed.

A: But it wouldn't be shop talk anymore, it would be ethnographic information. And if the professors were conscious of themselves as savage subjects, even they might stop talking (shop talking).

B: A blessed event, the coming of the ethnographer to the ingrown conversations of the closed shop—"To see ourselves as others see us" (Burns). And more blessed still should she come to the smug halls of twenty-first century academe. Enlightened halls, open—or so we citizens like to think—to every kind of talk.

A: And so they are.

B: Only if the talk is framed in a certain way. On our echoing green cultural memory is an object of devotion. Its two gods, or two-personed god, are science (positive knowledge, so to say) and philology (the knowledge of what is known). It's a cognitive scene, a scene of calculations and reflections. To the young in one another's arms—(that's to say, talking on their cellphones, text messaging) philology is the country for old men and old women of all ages. If young people come at all, it's to take the vacation called College.

B. After the imprisonment called high school... and the Earthly Paradise called primary school, where they came, before that, trailing clouds of glory.

C: Whatever. They don't come here because the knowledge of the young is mostly experiential, not reflective.

B: So there's Socrates in his trance and Alcibiades in his cups?

C: They will do nicely. Each in his way justifies and threatens every symposium, every state—the Outsiders nurtured from within. Admired and hated, sought and shunned; finally—because every state, every closed shop, is what it is—mysteriously disappeared.

B: And what then of your ethnographer, that darling of the modern academy? Isn't the ultimate dream of Wissenschaft that all things should submit to reflection, that experience itself should become—field work?

A: In the ancient world of Plato, that sick dream appeared as the Socratic philosopher. More recently it came as the nightmare of the positive scientist, mystified forever in the figure of Wordsworth's Newton, "voyaging through strange seas of thought, alone." Mary Shelley lifted his mask and we glimpsed the haunted face as Victor Frankenstein, whose monstrous creature is the index of Frankenstein's soul observed through the lens of an outsider's—in this case, a woman's—sense of the pitiful.

C: So you don't care for ethnographers either.

B: Well, they are our latest Faustian types. Benevolent colonialists. Today their shop talk—it's also called Cultural Studies—has brave new forms of self-mystification. As if the academy could harbor within itself its own outsider, its own critical observer!

A: That "critical observer" you imagine is the real illusion, isn't it? All observers—look at us!—are inside the shop. If we weren't we wouldn't even know about the shop, couldn't see it, and so couldn't talk at all. Shop talk is "interesting" when people can share their differences.

C: So for you it's not merely that "The only interesting talk is shop talk." For you, "Shop talk is all there is!"

A: Exactly. But some shop talk is more interesting than other shop talk.

C: And what makes it more interesting?

A: Every shop has many conversations going on inside it all the time. The most interesting conversations are those that get everybody else talking—talking about them, or talking in their terms.

B: But where do those new and interesting conversations come from? Inside the shop?

A: Evidently.

C: Why "evidently"? Is the rapt Socrates inside or outside? And what about Alcibiades—drunk or sober? We all remember how and where he died.

B: Inside or outside, it doesn't matter. (And by the way, we aren't at all certain where and how he died!)

A: Pedant.

B: The point is that every shop must be something other than what anyone, inside or outside, could think or imagine it to be. The shop must be, in some sense, beside itself. Irrational. Otherwise it can't accommodate anything "new."

A: Put it that way if you like. Shop talk is often irrational. Just so you don't bore me with a critical theory. Didn't the Poet say, "When a man talks to me of his theory, I let him talk" (Byron)?

B: He said system, not theory. But have it so if you like. Just so you don't insult me with ideas about knowing or accommodating otherness. No shop—no academy—can do that. Otherness comes like a wolf to a sheepfold. Later, when the damage is done, the priests indulge their shop talk of explanations.

Academiana

"It's a sheep eat sheep world."

"We will advance funeral by funeral."

Shop Talk (fragment of a lexicon)

Heteronormativity
Transgressive; transgress; transgression
Challenge (as verb)
Re-order the parameters
Contest; contestatory; contestation
Hegemony; hegemonic
Privilege (as verb)
Subversive
Hybridity (hybridization)
Rubricate
Horizon
temporality
trajectory
Foreground (as verb)
Bracket (as verb)
Reify; reification
Second order

Interestingly
One knows that
I want to show that
Liminal
paradigm
Enlist
Subaltern
carnavalesque
Valorize; valorization
Alterity
Hybridity
paramaterization
Problematize; problematic (unproblematic)
Imbricate; imbrication
Suture
Commodify, commodification
Recuperate
Essentialize

In the Beginning was the Word

Every critic who is worth his salt makes use of some particular clue-word of his own, some invoking symbolical keyword which serves him as his particular *Open Sesame*. I don't say he invents the word himself. As a rule he steals it. But he makes it his own and often makes more of it than its inventor did. My own favorite passwords of this sort are the word "secret," invented by Matthew Arnold; the word "life-illusion," invented by Ibsen; and finally the word "stupid being" invented by Gertrude Stein.

—John Cowper Powys, *Dostoyevsky*

LOSS. An ancient word of power, Loss began its Modern resurrection—its eternal return—in the late eighteenth- and early nineteenth-centuries. It named a force come to meet the coming of another set of forces named with the same word but ranged under the heading "economics": labor, wages, gain, money, commodities, utility. Within the sphere of this political economy, the word Loss was assigned the task of sustaining a specific system for creating wealth through a disciplined pursuit of rational self-interest.

That historical situation called from the dark backward and abysm of time three more primal forms of Loss. The first of these was forged by the antinomian gnostic visionary William Blake. Blakean Loss—that is to say, Loss unlinked to a system of rewards or utility—comes in his 1793 comic masterpiece *The Marriage of Heaven and Hell*, where he began to work out his visions of an economics of excess. A decade and more later he delivered an elaborated presentation of what he came to call "the Buildings of Los."

Briefly, the Buildings of Los are all the forms of a mortal world and universe—in Blake's view, the creations of a human imagination. These "productions of Time" emerge as a recreative response to the forces destroying the proper state of human life—i.e., the state of limitless desire.

> Earth was not: nor globes of attraction
> The will of the Immortal expanded
> Or contracted his all flexible senses.
> Death was not, but eternal life sprung
> —*The* [First] *Book of Urizen*

This universal condition is thrown into disorder when Primal Being turns in fear from its own desire. Imagined in dark biblical forms and named by Blake Urizen, this fearful Being invents the restricted economics of loss and gain. In Blake's view, this dismal science of Loss is realized in both the new system of "political economy" as well as in its religious precursor, the dialectics of Ancient Law ("holiness") and Christian redemption from law ("the days of futurity").

> From the depths of dark solitude. From
> The eternal abode in my holiness,
> Hidden set apart in my stern counsels
> Reserv'd for the days of futurity,
> I have sought for a joy without pain,
> For a solid without fluctuation
> Why will you die O Eternals?
> Why live in unquenchable burnings?

That passage describes the dreadful Book of Life and Loss as conceived and written by Primal Being bound to what Blake called, in the title of *The Four Zoas*, "the torments of love and jealousy."

The Buildings of Los emerge to unedit that dreadful book. These buildings are a perpetuated and living ruin—Loss—built on the fixed and dead ruins created by the tormented desires of the Urizenic world. This remarkable myth of Loss is distinctly post-Christian, a ruin razed from the Christian economy of grace. It is most fully worked out in the first chapter of Blake's *Jerusalem* where Los presides over the construction of the city of Los, Golgonooza.

> He views the City of Golgonooza, & its smaller Cities:
> The Looms & Mills & Prisons & Work-houses of Og & Anak:
> The Amalekite: the Canaanite: the Moabite: the Egyptian:
> And all that has existed in the space of six thousand years:
> Permanent, & not lost not lost nor vanishd, & every little act,
> Word, work, & wish, that has existed, all remaining still
> In those Churches ever consuming & ever building by the Spectres

Of all the inhabitants of Earth wailing to be Created
—Jerusalem

These are labors of decreation set in operation by the will of Los, the Will to Loss. It is a machinery introduced into the "spectrous" and illusory system of restricted desires, reversing its deadly consequences: "as cogs / Are formd in a wheel, to turn the cogs of the adverse wheel" (Milton).

Loud roar my Furnaces and loud my hammer is heard:
I labour day and night, I behold the soft affections
Condense beneath my hammer into forms of cruelty
But still I labour in hope, tho' still my tears flow down.
That he who will not defend Truth, may be compelld to defend
A Lie: that he may be snared and caught and snared and taken
That Enthusiasm and Life may not cease: arise Spectre arise!
Thus they contended among the Furnaces with groans & tears;
Groaning the Spectre heavd the bellows, obeying Los's frowns;
Till the Spaces of Erin were perfected in the furnaces
Of affliction, and Los drew them forth, compelling the harsh Spectre.
Into the Furnaces & into the valleys of the Anvils of Death
And into the mountains of the Anvils & of the heavy Hammers
Till he should bring the Sons & Daughters of Jerusalem to be
The Sons & Daughters of Los
—Jerusalem

This is a System of perpetuated Loss that "deliver[s] Individuals from... Systems" of illusory loss (*Jerusalem*). Its logic is sympathetic: to give "a body to Falshood that it may be cast off for ever" (*Jerusalem*); or,

That whenever any Spectre began to devour the Dead,
He might feel the pain as if a man gnawd his own tender nerves.
—Jerusalem

In face of this paradoxical work, a voice of doubt and despair continually asks: "Why wilt thou give to her a

Body whose life is but a Shade?" And that repeated doubt is met by the repetition of the need for Loss:

> And Los said. I behold the finger of God in terrors...
> Yet why despair! I saw the finger of God go forth
> Upon my Furnaces, from within the Wheels of Albions Sons:
> Fixing their Systems, permanent: by mathematic power
> Giving a body to Falshood that it may be cast off for ever.
> With Demonstrative Science piercing Apollyon with his own bow!
> God is within, & without! he is even in the depths of Hell!
>
> —*Jerusalem*

The pertinence of Blake's thought for a post-Enlightenment world is apparent in the many related forms of Loss that have caught the attention of Western minds during the past 200 years. One thinks immediately of the disciplines of Void-Enlightenment pursued in Buddhist philosophy—and perhaps most impressively in Nagarjuna's celebrated concept of "Emptiness" (*Sunyata*). Blake's verse and Nagarjuna's logic use very different means to work through and toward a similar end: human sympathy. Both are motivated by a deep compassion for human suffering, which they perceive as grounded in illusions about self-identity and the nature of the living world.

Equally pertinent are the "visions of excess" of Georges Bataille, to whom Blake is often compared. But much closer to Bataille is the experience of Loss first put into play by Byron and thence elaborated in the long line of Byronic inheritors. This is a second early response to bourgeois political economy—a response in this case generated not from a gnostic critique of religion but from an aristocrat's vision of the supercession of his class. For Byron, there is nothing to choose between Loss and Gain since both are regulated as a game of chance: "In play, there are two pleasures for your choosing, / The one is winning, and the other, losing" (*Don Juan*). Here all that matters is the "play," the immediate event which can be stopped (by death) but never concluded.

Neither Byron nor Bataille exhibit the kind of systematic and ethical concerns that clearly underlie the work of Blake (and Nagarjuna). Bataille's work is in fact a kind of anti-philosophy. After all, his most important philosophic works are works of fiction. Contradiction, including self-contradiction, forms the heart of his work—which is more a continuous act of writing than it is a philosophical or religious position. The similarity to Byron is apparent:

> If people contradict themselves, can I
> Help contradicting them, and every body,
> Even my veracious self?—But that's a lie;
> I never did so, never will—how should I?
> He who doubts all things, nothing can deny;
> Truth's fountains may be clear, her streams are muddy,
> And cut through such canals of contradiction,
> That she must often navigate o'er fiction.
>
> —*Don Juan*

Byron's life work, comical as well as desperate, is "to meditate amongst decay, and stand / A ruin amidst ruins" (*Childe Harold's Pilgrimage*). He fashions examples of how one may live and even thrive in a permanent condition of ruin and apparent hopelessness.

Finally, standing athwart Blakean and Byronic loss—at that epochal Western moment—was and still is Wordsworthian Loss. This is what Blake, a shrewd reader of Wordsworth, called "the lamentations of

Beulah." Wordsworth records for us the last ditch stand of the belief in traditional redemptive Loss:

> That time is past,
> And all its aching joys are now no more,
> And all its dizzy raptures. Not for this
> Faint I, nor mourn nor murmur; other gifts
> Have followed; for such loss, I would believe,
> Abundant recompence.
> —"Lines Composed a Few Miles Above Tintern Abbey"

The phrase "I would believe," as Wordsworth's greatest commentators have noted, tells the deep truth of Wordsworth's fierce and fragile faith. "Not without hope we suffer and we mourne": the double negative defines the bleak but determined assent entailed in Wordsworthian Loss.

> Not for a moment could I now behold
> A smiling sea, and be what I have been:
> The feeling of my loss will ne'er be old;
> This, which I know, I speak with mind serene.
>
> Then, Beaumont, Friend! who would have been the Friend,
> If he had lived, of Him whom I deplore,
> This work of thine I blame not, but commend;
> This sea in anger, and that dismal shore.
>
> O 'tis a passionate Work!—yet wise and well,
> Well chosen is the spirit that is here;
> That Hulk which labours in the deadly swell,
> This rueful sky, this pageantry of fear!
>
> And this huge Castle, standing here sublime,
> I love to see the look with which it braves,
> Cased in the unfeeling armour of old time,
> The lightning, the fierce wind, the trampling waves.

—"Elegiac Stanzas Suggested by a Picture of Peele Castle
in a Storm, Painted by Sir George Beaumont"

There is the faith of one committed to lose the whole world in order to gain—to save—the immortal soul he inherited from "the dead but sceptred sovereigns who still rule / Our spirits from their urns" (*Manfred*).

Toronto Star

Part I.

1. It all fell out of thinking
    I might at least be able to save myself
2. Some time all at once the idea struck me like a flash
    Rigging a beam with a pulley at the top of the house
3. and a rope leading to the ground I tied an empty barrel on one
    end of
    the rope pulled it to the top of the house and fastened
4. Then the rope's other end to a tree I climbed
    Back once again to the top I filled the barrel
    With lots of heavy bricks then I returned for the last time down
5. The stairs and I set the rope at the bottom end
    Finally loose from the tree and immensely pleased with myself
    I brought the barrel back however
    It happened I forgot

Part II.

6. Unfortunately that the barrel of bricks was now heavier than I
    was I knew
7. What was happening
    The barrel jerked me off
    The ground however I kept a tight hold of
    The rope and I met halfway up the barrel
8. Coming down I received a sharp blow to the left shoulder and
    then continued up
9. Banging my head
    right on the beam
    and jamming my fingers in the pulley when the barrel hit the
    ground
    the bottom just exploded
    and the bricks suddenly all burst out completely breaking up
    as I now to my horror found myself
10. Heavier than the barrel I simply started back
    In the other direction I gained more speed and met the blasted
    barrel

Halfway down and coming fast and all in pieces I was even a bit
relieved
At these final blows I found myself

Part III

11. Hopelessly confused because I dropped the rope the barrel itself
came
On my head I woke up coming in this hospital
12. You I trust will therefore understand
and please entertain this request for my sick leave.

On Sentimental and "Second-rate" Poetry in the Twentieth Century. (7/18/97)

I partly wrote *Poetics of Sensibility* because I learned about verse from my mother. When I was a boy she recited to me the verse of Hemans, Landon, Bryant, etc. Especially Longfellow because her family was from the Maritimes, which gave her a special love for "Evangeline." But the entire tradition of sentimental literature was available to her.

I mention this because it points to an important historical fact: that standards of taste and judgment are framed differently at different times and in different places. That thought—an academic commonplace—we academics often profess in bad faith, and never more so when it comes to setting up a *gradus ad parnassum*. When a commitment to poetry shifts from the Common Reader to the Professional, those differences tend to lose their force and value. Because profession-als—experts—are rather inclined to take their own views for the truth. But for a scholar it should be impossible to think our twentieth-century masters of taste in art and poetry—ourselves—are or were more dependable (or less) than Charles Eliot Norton or Anna Jamison etc. (or I than my mother!). We all acquire different preferences, of course, but that's what they are. So the book was in part an attempt to think and feel in sympathy with ways of thinking and feeling that have not been our ways, and to use our academic ways of talking to try to recover a sympathy with those other ways, now so lost to us (to our cost).

It seems to me essential that a poem like Joyce Kilmer's "Trees" be made recoverable. We may finally prefer other poems, but if we have no ability to sympa-thize with that work and works like it, we have confessed not a strength but a great weakness. Read Brooks and Warren on the poem again—their famous New Critical reading that sent the poem to oblivion. They thought it wasn't a very good poem. (But remem-ber—they also thought it *was* a poem, and as such worth exploring.) Myself, I don't agree with the way they read it—or at any rate, I have other ways. Or read Charles Bernstein's travesty/reading of the song "Shenandoah": there's sympathy for you! Do we actu-ally think we have a better sense of Ossian than Goethe had, or Byron, or any number of people of that period who found Ossian an exhaustless source? As they say these days, "be real."

My mother never wrote commentaries on poems or gave them interpretations. She memorized and recited the poems she loved.

Recitation Considered as a Fine Art

Any man of mechanical talents may, from the writings of Derrida or Jacques Lacan, produce ten thousand volumes of equal value with Aristotle's, and from those of Dante or Shakespeare an infinite number. But when he has done this, let him not say that he knows better than his master, for he only holds a candle in sunshine.

—William Blake,
The Marriage of Heaven and Hell, variant text

And 'tis my faith that every poem,
Enjoys the air I breathe.

—William Wordsworth,
"Lines Written in Early Spring," variant text

As we know, students—most ordinary and intelligent people, for that matter—imagine poems are difficult, full of deep meanings that have to be deciphered. It's our fault—we educators—that this dismal and quite mistaken view prevails. We've imagined that our proud schools of criticism have more to show us than the poetry itself. Above every poem we have inscribed a hellish warning: Abandon hope, all you who enter here.

As Gertrude Stein would say, we've got to begin again at the beginning, which is where poetry always locates itself anyway. For poetry is more like music than it is like fiction. Remember, novels emerged out of traditions of moral instruction. You don't memorize novels, you think about their worlds and you learn their lessons. But you do memorize poetry.

Why is that? Well, think about Edward Lear, about Dr. Seuss, about Blake's "Songs." We read "The Pelican Chorus" or "The Jumblies" to our children and they run over with laughter and happiness.

In Xanadu, on the hills of the Chankly Bore, before ever we ate of the tree of the knowledge of good and evil, we speak an Adamic language. When we memorize poems we re-imagine the practice of that language.

But before you can memorize you have to do your lessons. You have to learn to recite.

To begin again, forget about the meanings, they come along for the ride (they come with the territory). The poem is a musical score written in our mother tongue. Our bodies are the instruments it was made for. Perform:

Make me thy lyre, even as the forest is...
Be thou me, impetuous one.

The poem will obey if you pay attention to what you're doing. Its mechanisms aren't difficult, even if they are amazingly flexible. They are as natural to us as speaking and singing. We learned them before we knew them, on the banks of the Derwent, in our mother's or our nurse's arms.

The basic structure is like a double helix—one strand is linguistic—a syntax and a semantics—the other is prosodic, made of rhythmical and acoustic units (metre and rhyme). We practice to discover their synchrony. The two play off each other, and while every poem permits a personal inflection of its elements, your freedom is constrained. That constraint is telling you to pay attention to what you're doing.

When you set out to perform a poem, you don't proceed willy-nilly. You try it out and test its possibilities. There will always be multiple possibilities. Eventually, in the act itself, you'll have to make a performance decision. When you do that you'll have something else to look at and think about. What was good about what you did, what wasn't. And so you can begin again.

As Gertrude Stein says, beginning again and again.

Postlapsarian Note: In my experience, many difficulties of meaning disappear when students begin to construct and perform recitations. Indeed, only then do many other significant difficulties of meaning begin to reveal themselves. (Perhaps in poetry we're always working to find those beginnings.) Recitation compels you to give a specific shape to the text's linguistic and prosodic relations. They can't speak the words until your mouth, your lungs, and—indeed—your whole body understands how to give them articulate shape so that someone else will also understand. It's not hard to do but it does take practice. And you have to pay attention. And the more you do it, the better you get.

Of course, poems have eaten of the tree of knowledge of good and evil. There aren't many masterpieces like Blake's "The Lamb." Most are, as The Poet said, "like the scorpion, girt by fire" (Byron). They have assayed the bitter-sweet of a Shakespearean fruit (Keats). Nonetheless, poetry proposes for its immediate object pleasure, not truth, and that commitment, as The Poet says, "has made all the difference" (Frost). It is why poetry, as the atheist Shelley precisely puts the matter, "redeems from decay the visitations of the divinity in man."

Philology in a New Key

> If we are asked: "Who made the world?" [and] if we reply, "Nobody made it" ...we will have only seemingly given an answer; in reality *we have rejected the question*. The questioner feels called upon to repeat his problem: "Then how did the world become as it is?" If now we answer, "It has not become at all," he will be really disturbed. This "answer" clearly repudiates the very framework of his thinking.
> —Suzanne K. Langer

YA: What is the nature of literature and its functions as they are characterized by the poststructuralist revolution in the western tradition?

J: The nature of literature in this context is to expose the comedy of scholarship and criticism. Any literature that does not do this threatens to become academic self-advertising. The function of literature is therefore to declare that philosophy of literature is either decadent or comical or both.

This approach is necessary, in the context of the so-called "poststructuralist revolution," because that "revolution" is an academic fantasy. Of course there have been, and are, writings since 1970 that undermine this fantasy, as well as the academic industries that support it.

YA: Would you not think this an anarchist idea? Would you deny the humanist contents of literature?

J: On the contrary, I think it a decidedly humanist idea. After all, it's this so-called "poststructuralst revolution" that has been promoting ideas like "the posthuman." And "anarchist" is just a bogeyword anyway. I'm with Cocteau here. Remember what he said when he was asked about his politics? "I'm a moderate anarchist."
The danger to human being, to individuals and to the common good, has always come from "systems" of one kind or another. As Laura Riding once wrote, "Anarchism is not enough"—but then, the "anarchism" she was talking about was an important ground feature of humane being.

And as to that, we could all do worse, these days, than to read again that remarkable book of hers—perhaps the most trenchant theoretical work of High Modernist thinking written in English.

YA: What is the status of the subject in the cognitive understanding of literature?

J: In that understanding, the status of the subject is difficult. In normal conditions, however, the subject is OK.

YA: What makes a work different from a text? How do you differ from Paul de Man regarding the status of a text?

J: Somebody or other, anybody, makes a work differ from a text, or doesn't. De Man makes a work different from a text, and so do I. But we make different differences. "Here comes everybody" (Joyce). Defining the differences—beyond those already made by different people—is somebody (anybody) else's business.

YA: You emphasize historical materiality over the de Manian stress on linguistic materiality. Are you not trying, in the words of Terry Eagleton, to bring aesthetic under "cognitive, ethical and political realms"? Are you not politicizing aesthetic?

J: Sometimes. So what? Does anyone think that "the aesthetic" is "not among the ideologies"? Marx, alas, imagined it wasn't. But as Our Lady of the Flowers told the judge at her trial: "We're already beyond that."

YA: I know you are an authority in your area. Let me ask what is your own method of reading a text?

J: Authority? As the bumper stickers say, never trust it, and least of all—as Socrates warned—when it's your own. Method? On this topic I think Byron has the last word: "When a man talks of system, his cause is hopeless." So let's leave a little room for hope.

YA: How does the act of reading which places the text as a part of an infinite labyrinth of intertexuality mark a shift from the work to text?

J: It doesn't. To think so is one of the silliest critical illusions of our ivory-tower time.

YA: As de Man points out, there are two modes of reading—aesthetically aware and rhetorically aware. Which one do you find compelling? Why?

J: There are as many modes of reading as there are events of reading. I think De Man must have said that to trick readers who study aesthetics and rhetoric. Why? Because his life's work was to confound the illusions of the critics. Alas, he came up short. He never thought to laugh at them.

YA: What constitutes ambivalence, indeterminacy, and the fluctuation of meaning in a text? How would you explain the incompatibility of grammatical and rhetorical structures? What constitutes the incompatibilities and indeterminacies of a text?

J: As Kathy Acker observes throughout *Empire of the Senseless*, it's not a question of "What," it's a question of "Who." Once you make that linguistic transformation, the problems of indeterminacy begin to seem the normal condition of our everyday lives.

YA: How does a rhetorical reading of a text differ from a grammatical one? Would you describe how each respective reading can be offered to the text? What are the limitations of each?

J: You ask three questions so here are three replies (in this kind of discussion, questions have replies, never answers):

1. Since the differences are not a priori but eventual, there is no answer to such a question—though as you see, one can reply to it.

2. If I did, the description would be misleading. So I will only say that different readings should be offered to a text with great respect. Too often critics and readers are like the Angels in Blake's *The Marriage of Heaven and Hell*, reading "as if they were the only wise. [And] They do this with a confident insolence sprouting from systematic reasoning." So Blake reminds us that when we read Dante or Shakespeare, "any man of mechanical talents" can produce an indefinite number of interpretations: "But when he has done this, let him not say that he knows better than his master, for he only holds a candle in sunshine."

3. They have no limitations beyond what you decide upon.

YA: What is the text after all—when we imagine, as we do these days, that "everything is text"? What are its textures and how can one—either a reader or an author—insert himself/herself in the textures of history and time?

J: 1. As Jesus said to Pilate, "Thou hast said it."

2. And as he (also) said to the Centurion, I say to the critic: "Sell all that you have, give to the poor, and come follow me."

YA: Who is the author of the text and what relationship does he share with the text, reader, meaning and the social world around?

J: Everyone and everything.

YA: How does the nature of language help the text resist its closure?

J: Easily. But sometimes people want to make things difficult for themselves and others. The difficulties can make for lots of fun.

YA: What role can you attribute to the discourse of cultural practice and to the role of language in forming the texture of our reality/truth and even our identities?

J: The problem with the question lies in the phrase "discourse of cultural practice." This is the jargon of the schools and its use promotes many illusions and fantasies in our academic world, as I've already suggested. But if we blow away the misty talk that has been choking us for years, I would say this: humanist scholars and educators have a single function—to preserve and pass on to the present and the future as much of our cultural inheritance as we can, and in as undamaged a form as we can. To do that well carries a corollary demand: that we preserve, protect, and defend the languages of our various worlds. This is the mission, the vocation, of the humane scholar and educator. "It's not rocket science," as one might say.

The Living Theatre

The Living Theatre of actors emerges
From the audience, as if each of us were only one
Of them. Wonderful to be so distinguished, an art
Beyond the reach of art. They come down to us
From several places to gather on an empty stage.
                                        At first they stretch
And exercise (are these actors at all we wonder? What
Will they play?), we watch politely, 10, 15, 20 minutes
Of their ordinary professional nothing. Finally
In shoes that make no sound, in a play without words,
An accompaniment of industrial noise. They begin.
They are strong and all can climb as dancers walk.
(For two hours they will display their bodies' expertise. They
have nothing to say, they represent the world in 19
68, that time they called it *Frankenstein*, their summing
up. Dismantling the last dramatic contraption, they begin
to climb. Economical figures rise on the bodies of others

standing below, hands and forearms interlock,
beings hanging in air like flying buttresses. All are dressed
in black leotards and dancing shirts. Further forms scramble
quickly up the steps of building forms, find their places, and
still no one speaks. In our passive seats we stare in
unbelief at these final people crawling to the top
of 40 feet of bodies, to the head or where a head
should be to form a face. The creature is accomplished, arms
out 30 feet or more in threat or crucifixion, the legs
more than human, more than any of us. And the face
we find appears a mechanical device and visual aid, a pair
of eyes burning red, large as klieg lights, it is
a tremendous grand illusion,

                                        a production of 20
08 random memories, a presence barely yet
an artifice in the grip of a bygone endurance.
Last week an old Chicago friend blew into town, stopped here,
We reminisced about that night the Living Theatre
Played the university, narrating a story that had grown
Into a legend. I added variants and notes and then we stopped.
There seemed nothing more to say until he said
"A couple of years ago a Professor I know explained
The Living Theatre as 'one of those peculiar
Phenomena of a disturbed time. Of course there was no
Question of its surviving a period when prophecies
Were everyday events. Now we know it as no more
Than 10 prose lines in a book about post-war drama,
The obligatory notice in a standard reference work.'
What do those words give back to anyone who wasn't there?"

Nothing now for someone else except a testimony:
"As the case was turned over upon the wharf, a rattling was
heard inside. The looking-glass was broken. The pieces were
wedge-shaped; the cracks radiated from the center, as if the
glass had been struck by a pointed instrument."

Part II
POINTED INSTRUMENTS

Yourcenar's Empire of the Sensuous*

Though she writes a limpid French prose, inviting translation, she is not easy, and no writer *des nos jours*. Doubtless there were moments when she would have sympathized entirely with Alfieri's bitter remark: "I had rather compose in a language almost dead, and for a people all but extinct." But her despair at the carelessness and wastage of her own world, while acute, was measured by her sense of pity at the spectacle, its long history, and the fragile spirits who stood against it. Her work is an effort to summon those spirits—the dead as well as the living.

But we must ask: *Why did she do this? To what purpose?* The questions are relevant because her work has little access to "a public more and more incapable of reading" (*Mishima*), as she was well aware.

Nearing the end of the 25-year pursuit of her masterpiece, *Memoirs of Hadrian*, Yourcenar saw clearly how far her work was diverging "from the kind of book, and of man, who would please the public" ("Reflections").

As to the man she chose to imagine in that remarkable book, he was one of Walter Benjamin's victors, and one without great vices to deplore or virtues to deconstruct. Hadrian was notably, deliber-

---

*The texts cited here are the translations produced in each case "in collaboration with the author," as the title pages of the books indicate: *Memoirs of Hadrian and Reflections on the Composition of Memoirs of Hadrian*, trans. Grace Frick (Farrar, Straus, Giroux: New York, 1963); *The Mighty Sculptor, Time*, trans. Walter Kaiser (Farrar Straus, Giroux: New York, 1992); *Mishima. A Vision of the Void*, trans. Alberto Manguel (Farrar Strauss Giroux, 1986). These translations closely reflect, and fairly represent, Yourcenar's French, which can be read in *Mishima ou la vision du vide* (Gallimard: Paris, 1980); *Oeuvres romanesques* (Gallimard: Paris, 1982); and *Le Tempts, ce grand sculpteur. essais.* (Gallimard: Paris, 1983).

ately unspectacular. As a man he traveled much and was curious, as the emperor his chief object was to preserve tranquility and the status quo. The *vox populi* of history, when it recalls him at all, remembers him in two relations: for the now ruined wall he had constructed across northern England to hold back troublesome Celts; and for his love of the youth Antinuous, about whom we know almost nothing except that he drowned when he was 20 years old and was said to be very beautiful.

And what kind of book did she write? Like all her works, a learned one, painstakingly constructed from a long process of scholarly research and personal reflection.

Nearing his death, an undemonstrative Roman emperor writes his memoir, an autobiographical letter to his adopted grandson Marcus Aurelius. The recollections are often pedestrian and even tedious—a quality in Hadrian's account that Yourcenar accentuates through the flattened and objective majesty of her prose. Few things stand out in special relief: every event and person, every place or thing, commands attention, according to the basic method of Tantric yoga which so attracted Yourcenar: "not *awakening* but *attention*" ("Approaches to Tantrism," *That Mighty Sculptor, Time*). As a result, historical time in this book—the shape of the Empire—morphs (not shrinks) to the shape of an individual life. And while Hadrian himself singles out four special events—his accession as emperor, his love of Antinuous, the campaign against the Jewish insurgents, and his imminent death—these finally serve but to delineate stages in Hadrian's monumentally quotidian experience: "all the mere routines of a life", as he laconically observes. They are less

important as events—*Memoirs of Hadrian* has virtually
no plot—than as what Coleridge would call "Aids to
Reflection."

In her own "Reflections of the Composition of
Memoirs of Hadrian" Yourcenar comments usefully on
how she wrote the book. This remark on general
method is especially interesting:

> The rules of the game: learn everything, read every-
> thing, inquire into everything, while at the same
> time adopting to one's ends the *Spiritual Exercises* of
> Ignatius of Loyola, or the method of Hindu ascetics,
> who for years, and to the point of exhaustion, try to
> visualize ever more exactly the images which they
> create beneath their closed eyelids.... Strive to read a
> text of the Second Century with the eyes, soul, and
> feelings, of the Second Century....

As Yourcenar knows, this game "to establish an unbro-
ken contact between Hadrian and ourselves" is a
scholar's art. Worse still, it is a game that must be lost
because "like the head of the *Mondragone Antinuous* in
the Louvre, [Hadrian and his world] are still living in a
past time, a time that has died." ("Reflections")

Only a scholar thinks that way. These dead are
alive precisely because, in the perspective of Yourcenar's
presence, they have died. They are not beings living in
a Christian afterlife, hell or purgatory or heaven. They
are living in a time that has died (which is not the same
thing as a time that is dead). This irrevocable condition
is what makes them dear, cherished in Yourcenar's
imaginings:

> One foot in scholarship, the other in magic arts, or,
> more accurately and without metaphor, absorption

in that *sympathetic magic* which operates when one transports oneself, in thought, into another body and soul.

—"Reflections"

Yourcenar's art is not meant to bring these creatures back to life, but to bring them back to the death they, like Yourcenar and ourselves, are both fated to endure.

We lose track of everything, and of everyone, even ourselves. The facts of my father's life are less known to me than those of the life of Hadrian. My own existence, if I had to write it, would be reconstructed by me from externals, laboriously, as if it were the life of someone else.... What is ever left but crumbled walls, or masses of shade? Here, where Hadrian's life is concerned, try to manage so that the lacunae of our texts coincide with what he himself might have forgotten.

—"Reflections"

"What is ever left but crumbled walls," like Hadrian's in far-off England? This text pivots on that sic transit commonplace exactly as *Memoirs of Hadrian* pivots on the four key events of the emperor's life. In each case what is most obvious is there to draw our attention to what is less obvious, though equally—if not even more—important. "My own existence, if I had to write it": that is to say, what Yourcenar *had to* write was the life of Hadrian, not her autobiography. "Here," then, the passage's themes of knowledge and self-knowledge flood back into that arresting aside about the book she had to write. The discipline of self-attention— Yourcenar's great and recurrent subject—is developed at the strange diagonal of a book like *Memoirs of*

Hadrian, where the pursuit of "the lacunae of our texts" becomes a spiritual exercise.

II.

Yourcenar died in 1987. A mere generation past, hers seems a faraway cultural world—a truly queer world, more distant in certain respects than imperial Rome was to her. The difference is not a matter of years but of temper, and the culminant section of *Memoirs of Hadrian*, "Patientia," indexes the difference. Like the films of Visconti, Yourcenar's writing is deliberate, unhurried, sensuous. Its quality is "the result of unceasing discipline" and a "maximum of attention" owed to every detail of experience ("Approaches to Tantrism"), and not least to the sensual dimensions of experience and awareness. Hence the quiet and sacramental *voluptas* with which Yourcenar invests Hadrian's last words: "Let us try, if we can, to enter into death with open eyes" (*Memoirs of Hadrian*). This is a pledge of allegiance as alien to a consumer society as one could imagine. Conjuring that ultimate act of awareness, Yourcenar is laying down, like Montaigne long ago, a standard for measuring how each moment of one's life should be lived.

Estranged from a public more and more incapable of reading, Yourcenar set herself apart from what she called "the mediocre, the false, and the prefabricated in literature produced for... the reading but unthinking masses, who expect a writer to give back to them their own image of the world" (*Mishima*). She does not discover that her books and subjects hold no interest for "the public," she decides that. For a writer, taking such a decision amounts to a kind of suicide.

And suicide would be one of her most preoccupying subjects, culminating in her study of the suicide, at once spectacular and absurd, of Yukio Mishima.

PRINTER'S DEVIL. *Please*, give me a break! Isn't the more pertinent question: why should we care about this proud woman and her pretentious works? The Emperor Hadrian, the incredibly successful right wing Japanese nationalist Yukio Mishima? Tantric Yoga and ritual suicide? Yourcenar's preoccupations are about as privileged as one could imagine. Truly, as Jesus might have said, she has had her reward. She was the first woman elected to the French Academy. Her works have been widely translated. And now she is enshrined in publishing heaven, La Bibliothèque de la Pléiade. Rest in peace.

Exactly, it's not about her, it's about us. Richardson, Proust, even Byron: where are the snows of yesteryear? "Gone—glimmering through the dream of things that were" (Byron).

PRINTER'S DEVIL. Huh?

Forget it.

PRINTER'S DEVIL. I guess I have.

But somebody hasn't forgotten and somebody shouldn't. Yourcenar isn't important because she's Important. She's important, like Hadrian's life, because now her high style seems so unimportant. Out of it, not just for the culture of *American Idol*, Reality TV, or *Sex and the City*. If Jane Austen, Henry James, and Robert Graves can be repackaged for movie and television consumption—even, we may think, with sometime success—*Memoirs of Hadrian* would be a stretch not worth the trouble to try, and *The Abyss* (*L'oeuvre au noir*, 1968, trans. 1976) unimaginable. The difference comes from the date of Yourcenar's elitism, the belatedness of a writing whose grand (or grandiose?) aspirations must seem—like Cervantes or Byron—either tragic or comic, depending how we sympathize with the demons of our demonic age.

Yourcenar's tragi-comedy comes through with special force in her little 1970 essay "The Sinister Ease of Dying." The occasion is the suicide of "several young people in Lille, in Paris, and, only a few months ago, in Provence" who "felt, rightly or wrongly, that they had only the choice of sacrificing to the false gods of avidity and violence among which we agree to live or else of protesting with their deaths" (*That Mighty Sculptor, Time*). Yourcenar's sympathy with their act is deep: "In one respect at least, they were not wrong: one cannot live without being implicated" (ibid.) Yourcenar underscores what our complicity involves in a harrowing and gorgeous periodic sentence.

> They quit a world in which wars more radically destructive than ever take place amidst a peace which isn't really peace and tends too often to become as destructive as war itself for man and his environment, a world in which advertisements for gastronomic restaurants stand side by side in the newspapers with accounts of people dead from hunger, where every woman who wears a fur coat contributes to the extinction of a living species, where our passion for speed aggravates every day the pollution of a world on which we depend for life, where every avid reader

of murder mysteries or of sinister news items and every spectator at films of violence contributes without knowing it to this passion for killing [sic? Without knowing it?] which has resulted in the millions of people put to death in the past half century.

PRINTER'S DEVIL. A prose as stylistically preposterous today as Faulkner's.

Much more preposterous. Because Yourcenar is closer to us, aware of her belatedness and aesthetic limits. And yet also factually, objectively true. And so doubly *true*: candid as well as accurate.

Asking then (of herself) whether "those young people [were] right or wrong to leave all that," Yourcenar first thinks that it would "depend on whether or not their sacrifice caused a change of heart in those around them" (*That Mighty Sculptor, Time*). But because she knows very well that these evils persist *in saecula seaculorum*, she moves to a different question: "can we in future prevent other pure hearts from following the same road?" Her response is to admit that "none of the usual reasons we might have given them for continuing to live are sufficiently compelling to restrain someone who can no longer tolerate the world as it is." Then she thinks of what she thinks to be an unusual reason: "One can usefully counterpoise only the tradition which claims that the Buddha himself, on the point of entering into peace, decided to remain in this world so long as one living creature needed his help."

But this reason is unusual only because it is framed as the wisdom of the Buddha. It is in fact a

commonplace reason—dare we say, *ancient wisdom*?—
that anyone would plead in such a case; and that many
have plead, often in vain, as we know. Invoking the
Buddha is a preposterous move, yes, though the reason
he enshrines remains a good reason, a loving reason.
Seizing it, Yourcenar finishes her essay:

> Perhaps we might have saved them if we had
> persuaded them that their refusal, their indignation,
> their very despair were necessary; if we had known
> how to urge against the sinister ease of dying the
> heroic difficulty of living—or of trying to live—in
> such a way as to make the world a little less scan-
> dalous than it is.

Another complex and beautiful sentence unfolds, this
time pivoting on the balanced rhetoric of "The sinister
ease of dying" and "the heroic difficulty of living" ("su
opposer cette facilité sinister de mourir la difficulté
héroïque de vivre"). Even these dreadful deaths draw
out a stylistic and literary ritual, as they drew out
Yourcenar's memory of the Buddha's legend. But are
aesthetic gestures what we want here? Is there not a
sinister ease of writing this way, of having acquired this
habit of Beauty? The essay's title and dominant theme,
taken from a poem by Victor Hugo reflecting on those
who died a century earlier in the Paris Commune, has
set Yourcenar on this learned course.

But Yourcenar's very eloquence teases us into
thought. The sinister *ease* of dying? The heroic (!) difficulty of living? Slogans are hovering everywhere
(Choose life, not Death). How dare think in these
ways, if thinking is what you care about? In that view,
the prose is ludicrous.

But how dare think, from that thought, that this is an easeful or heroic writing? There is a sinister ease in such critical thinking, and one grown as familiar with us today as Yourcenar was familiar with the art of language.

Yourcenar's artful prose will not "make death clear or make life durable," as the poet has written (Swinburne). But it does bring clarity to an engagement with her terrible subject. Part of that clarity is the exposure of the limits of her own writing. "Perhaps we might have saved them." The modesty of the remark carries us to reflect further: Perhaps, but not likely. And what did we expect anyway, answers? Take the artifice instead, Yourcenar's "way... to make the world a little less scandalous than it is."

If it isn't much, it is something, quite something—the glory of the miniscule gestures of art, beautiful and effectual in the only way that art can matter. Yourcenar makes the point even more explicitly in another, earlier essay, "Oppian, or The Chase" (1956). Here she recovers for close inspection an ancient poem about hunting, the *Cynegetica* ("The Chase"), from "that now dead genre of didactic works in verse which was esteemed through all antiquity" and beyond, "throughout the Middle Ages and into the Renaissance" of Buffon and others. Long believed the work of "Oppian, a Greek from Cilicia... at the time of Commodus," we now know its actual author was someone else, "another Greek poet, who was born in Apamea on the Orontes and was a contemporary of Caracalla." Yourcenar tracks the passage of this obscure work "come down to us through some twenty manuscripts scattered in various European libraries," thence through its several Latin translations, and finally to

Florent Chrestien's French translation edited and published by him in 1575 and "dedicated to Henri de Navarre, who loved hunting."

Yourcenar, we know, did not love hunting. But because nothing human was alien to her imagination, the love of hunting preserved in a poem that died long ago offered a special challenge.

A bookish world traveler, Yourcenar "admire[s] the superimposed layers of thought, experience, and labor out of which those old books which have come down to us are composed." Her admiration grows intense and very physical, tracking "the love of venery" across various spaces and times of the Mediterranean and Near Eastern world down to the particular object that set her imagination going in the first place.

> A Greek poet who lived in Asia around the 245th Olympiad was edited in Paris in 1555 by a Renaissance scholar. The ancient roll of parchment, wrapped in red silk and rolled on a rod of ivory, became, through the intermediary of medieval manuscripts, the volume printed in Greek with handsome characters engraved by Claude Garamond which reproduce the script of the Cretan Vergetios, the king's calligrapher.

Beautiful? No doubt. But by any ordinary measure, even the ordinary measures of the academy we serve, a queer devotion, an inconsequent work. Yet when we watch Yourcenar giving her attention to this book and searching out its rich "superimposed layers of thought," which of us do not examine the conscience of our own scholarly interests and pursuits?

There is more. "If you leaf through this text," Yourcenar goes on to say, "you will feel yourself taken out of dates and history and transported into a universe which knows the alternation of night and day and the passing of seasons but is ignorant of the clock of centuries." A student of that clock, Yourcenar seeks the talismanic power of these books, these *things*, to enter into the immediacy of the life they sustain.

> Here is this world, at once older and younger than we, new at each dawn, which man has decimated and abused since the time of hunters in chlamydes or jerkins, who had at least the excuse of believing in the inexhaustible abundance of nature, an excuse we no longer have—we who not only continue to destroy animals but work to annihilate nature itself. Here is this world we rediscover with a beating heart every time we go for a walk at dawn.

The force of the text lies in its frankly imaginative status: "Here is this world." A god-gifted natural order returns to us "Here" in Yourcenar's prose.

We have come to cherish these self-reflexive gestures in our works of art. So from this belated moment in our Enlightenment heritage, academically sustained, we read those kinds of imaginative moves as especially provident, even redemptive. But this is just what Yourcenar will not permit. Here in this prose Yourcenar brings back the natural world exactly as she brought back the world of Hadrian: on one hand "a time that has died," on another a world that is dying, more "decimated and abused" than ever. Imagination here does not redeem, it reveals. It tells the truth, including the truth about itself, and its office is to serve the world "as in itself it really is": not to imagine empty illusions but to empty out the illusions we live to imagine.

And do not mistake Yourcenar's candor. This is her Song of Innocence—discovering a dawn rising upon the nature we continue to abuse. The loss being marked is not nature's, whose inhuman glories will mutate and persist; the loss is ours, which Yourcenar must share even as she rises up against it, dawn to dawn.

> "Sing of human unsuccess/In a rapture of distress"
> —Auden

III.

When Matthew Arnold dismissed Shelley as "a beautiful and ineffectual angel," he was arguing, like Plato long ago, that poetry had to justify itself before the interests of the state. But those interests are ideological, that is to say, as various and shifting as the Culture Wars that feed and sustain them. Ministers of culture—ourselves—struggle in these wars, promoting and defending ideas that we judge, as best we can, what is good, right, just. Imitating and revealing the world, poets inevitably participate in those wars.

The decision to participate "in imagination" is consequential. It is to labor in a kind of Cassandra's vision, which Arnold deplored as a cursed poetic state where "everything is to be endured, and nothing to be done." But for the poet, Cassandra's is a vision of truth in the midst of a world riven by illusion. Her efforts to ward off disaster are struggles—enduring and ineffectual—against the sinister ease of the dying she sees all around her. The enduring ineffectuality of poetry is thus the form of its greatest truth—a truth that the world of getting and spending dare not imagine or speak.

That truth is perhaps most clearly exposed in a scholar's art like Yourcenar's. Or rather, it may be most clearly exposed for scholars and critics, who devote ourselves to culture and heritage. But to what should we give our devotion? The best that has been known and thought? Walter Benjamin's losers?

Do we even know what or who these are? Oppian? Shakespeare? There is a time for every purpose under heaven.

Besides, it is all decimated and abused and, as ancient wisdom observes, "has been and will be again." Trotsky called the knowledge of these things "the privilege of historical backwardness."

An Ax for the Frozen Sea

Wierdly and for ever rises up the rabble of the machines.
They multiply like rabbits, they come from the mills of generation.
      Where are they going now?
Not to love, not to the factories of happiness.

Once again the men pour out, faithless and vain. Creation groans,
and love, too fit for them to give and to receive.
In an idiotic pride they think about the meaning of love
though they were closer to that truth when they worshipped cruel gods

and knew the nothing that belongs to men and to those gods.
The world has always served the sciences of the artificial
and was first possessed by stones, too wise to speak
      of this any more.

Perverse men say the stones will speak again.
      But they will not.
Do we dare escape in abandonment to the charm of impossible objects?
Adam spoke with beasts when they were very young.

And now many are dumb as brick or steel.
Others in a furious catastrophe hum or buzz, resisting wisdom.
Innocent birds or roaring lions willing or unwilling,
all shall come to have their tongues torn out, like saints.

To conceive this now stirs panic. Nonetheless, the machines, with men,
      are running out of time as quickly as possible.
They do not know this but they will.
Men of sympathy and imagination distrust the thought of their machines.

But there is no need, why be anxious, listen.
Do you hear the rust? No one is laughing at death.
The buildings are lost in silence when we have disappeared.

What are you holding on to after all? The world is free.
A fine dust is settling and the past waits for you.
When the winds vanish there is all that desolation.

Horizons watch the moveless flats,
the machines fall into starry darkness with no end in sight,
where love finds its place in this bewilderment.

Say nothing. Look. Someone is playing.
Fire the mind point blank into the eyes of the mind.
A black hole does not see and does not send. It holds the light.

To Hans Gumbrecht, in the Wilderness

Nel mezzo del cammin di nostra vita
mi ritrovai per una selva oscura
ché la diritta via era smarrita.

—Dante, *Inferno*

William Blake addressed his last poetical work, *The Ghost of Abel*, "To Lord Byron, in the Wilderness" (1822). It is a mini drama reflecting on Byron's just published play *Cain*, which was the last straw of Byron's wickedness for many English readers—as he was amused to realize: "But Juan was my Moscow, and Faliero / My Leipsic, and my Mont Saint Jean seems Cain" (*Don Juan*).

Blake's response was more thoughtful than the outraged reviews. I'm not so much concerned with what his skit might be taken to *mean*, however, as to point out two interesting facts about it. First, if it is what it seems to be—a critical interpretation of Byron and his play—its aesthetic condition necessarily deforms any expository meaning—that's to say, any interpretation—we might want to extract from it. Second, the pointed dedication "To Lord Byron, in the Wilderness" involves a personal reference to a little allegory Blake composed some thirty-years earlier about the tormented "Just Man," who "rages in the wilds where lions roam" because "Now the sneaking serpent" of debased religion is the prince of the spiritual world.

Both of those facts are relevant to what I'd like to say about Hans Gumbrecht's recent book *Production of Presence* (2004). Gumbrecht seems to me a tormented Just Man raging in the wilderness of contemporary culture. His torment is revealed in his book, which itself proposes an end to the torment it is trying to diagnose. Writing as he does, however, Gumbrecht is surrounded by, wrapped into, and perhaps even mediated by "clouds and cushions of [the conceptual] meaning" he is trying to escape.

I. Concluding Unscientific Prescript

Production of Presence is an expository pamphlet so let's engage it first on its own terms, with an expository translation that might answer to Gumbrecht's imprisoned prose.

PRINTER'S DEVIL: That prose is distinctly not what "the Age demanded" (Pound). Give me something more like Blake's response to Byron—a *Prose pour le transiberien*, for instance! (Cendrars)

    Production of Presence is a learned polemic urging students of literature and culture to step back and away from hermeneutics, or what he calls "meaning culture," as the ground of their critical and scholarly work. Not to abandon it altogether, but to observe and study its serious limitations. Briefly, Gumbrecht argues that an interpretive procedure based in a hermeneutic approach to meaning produces a culture of abstractions. He urges us to install a more materially-oriented approach to value and meaning. In place of a program that "gives a higher value to the meaning of phenomena than to their material presence" he urges a more direct approach to value and meaning. Gumbrecht wants interpretive "concepts that would allow us to point to what is irreversibly nonconceptual in our lives."

That is a large philosophical and ethical proposal. Gumbrecht's focus, however, is yet more pointed. He is interested in art and poetry, in forms of expression that are in themselves presence-oriented— aesthetic, operating at a level Blake called "the doors of perception." Indeed, although Gumbrecht never mentions Blake, he might well have put this famous passage from *The Marriage of Heaven and Hell* over the entrance to his book:

> If the doors of perception were cleansed every thing
> would appear to man as it is, Infinite.
> For man has closd himself up till he sees all things
> through the narrow chinks of his cavern.

That would be for Blake the cavern of the embrained soul, which has lost a full intellectual existence. Like Gumbrecht, Blake imagines that "an improvement of sensual enjoyment" (*The Marriage of Heaven and Hell*) will help us escape from "The Human Abstract" we become when we embrace "meaning culture" instead of "presence culture."

Gumbrecht is committed to the revelatory and even redemptive capacities of "aesthetic experience" as a means to a fully-realized "lived experience." We glimpse that ideal state when "objects of aesthetic experience... are characterized by an oscillation between presence effects and meaning effects." However, this ideal has been attenuated "under contemporary cultural conditions" where meaning-culture dominates our experience. In such a state "presence culture" turns fleeting, pitched into darkness and evanishment:

> Presence phenomena cannot help being inevitably
> ephemeral, cannot help being what I call "effects of

presence"—because we can only encounter them within a culture that is predominantly a meaning culture. For us, presence phenomena always come as "presence effects" because they are necessarily surrounded by, wrapped into, and perhaps even mediated by clouds and cushions of meaning.

II.

"I now mean to be serious—it is time"

—Byron

But *Production of Presence* necessarily produces the wilderness of the meaning culture it is trying to dismantle. This happens because the book is sleeping among the clouds and cushions of abstract thought—the ideas and concepts of interpretation pursued by all those philosophers, not least among them Heidegger, the philosopher's philosopher. What is Gumbrecht *doing* among the fleshpots of philosophy, empty as they must necessarily be of the sustenance he desires? He appears to know a truth that cannot set him free:

> Poetry is perhaps the most powerful example of the simultaneity of presence effects and meaning effects—for even the most overpowering institutional dominance of the hermeneutic dimension could never fully repress the presence effects of rhyme and alliteration, of verse and stanza.

Just so. Vorwärts, Gumbrecht! Aber, was ist dies?

> It is telling, however, that literary criticism has never been able to react to the emphasis that poetry gives to such formal aspects—except for the estab-

lishment of long, boring, and intellectually pointless "repertoires" that list, in chronological order, the different poetic forms within different national literatures, and except for the "theory of over-determination," which claims, against all immediate evidence, that poetic forms will always double and reinforce already existing meaning structures. The intuition, in contrast, that instead of being subordinated to meaning, poetic forms might find themselves in a situation of tension, in a structural form of oscillation with the dimension of meaning, turned out to be another promising starting point toward a general reconceptualization of the relationship between effects of meaning and effects of presence.

Oh dear—a "starting point toward a general reconceptualization, etc." I thought all this was a march toward something "irreversibly nonconceptual." "Into the Valley of Death / Rode the Six hundred" (Tennyson).

FOOTNOTE: And might it be noted that the history of "literary criticism"—even into our Age of Bronze—*has often been able to react to the emphasis that poetry gives to such formal aspects* as Gumbrecht rightly prizes. Just to stay on the American scene, Poe's supremely ludic "The Philosophy of Composition" starts a tradition that has continued to our own day in works like Howe's (distinctly non-ludic) *My Emily Dickinson* and the mixed messages of Bernstein's *Artifice of Absorption*—among many others.

As a starting point we need, let's say, a general deconceptualization not a general reconceptualization. Clearing the decks. We are about to cross a dangerous intersection so first of all pay attention to your Mother Tongue: Stop, look, listen. Is the coast clear?

> The coast—I think it was the coast that I
> Was just describing—Yes, it was the coast—
> *—Don Juan*

If it's the example of poetry we want, take me to the river, drop me in the water.

> The Promise in Disturbance
> How low when angels fall their black descent,
>   Our primal thunder tells: known is the pain
> Of music, that nigh throning wisdom went,
>   And one false note cast wailful to the insane.
>   Now seems the language heard of Love as rain
> To make a mire where fruitfulness was meant.
>   The golden harp gives out a jangled strain,
> Too like revolt from heaven's Omnipotent.
> But listen in the thought; so may there come
>   Conception of a newly-added chord,
> Commanding space beyond where ear has home.
> In labour of the trouble at its fount,
>   Leads Life to an intelligible Lord
> The rebel discords up the sacred mount.

Why this poem? Why not? We don't need a *reason* for it, we need an experience—as unprepared as possible. This is always the way we want to begin—with as little pre-reading as we can manage to slip past.

Besides, it's a genuinely *philosophical* poem— George Meredith's little manifesto for writing sonnets to a "jangled strain" of verse.

Observe that while the poem is evidently taking up very big ideas, it continually short circuits a conceptual or expository translation. So try forgetting about what it might be taken to mean, look at how it works. I give just two examples, one from the beginning, and one from the ending:

1. The very first line *falls* out of prose and disturbs our reading. So we work at the line and decide there's an inversion. And we translate: "How low the black descent of angels when they fall." Which is fine except the line is so constructed that it keeps teasing us out of that de-deformative idea and back to the poem's straightforward transitive form—its first literality. Of course nobody *wants* the verb "fall" to operate transitively, but here it is made to behave as if it were (O that Meredithian rag!), as if it wanted to. And why shouldn't it work that way since the angels, as the old stories aver, chose wicked ways from the beginning.

And then consider for a moment the "fleeting presence" we feel that the phrase "How low" might signal either a question or an exclamation. When we translate we learn (don't we?) from somebody called "primal thunder" what "How low" really *means*. (But once we have imagined the possibilities of those other meanings, what are we going to do? Forget about them? The Great Tempter—he's roaming all around this poem—knows how to play with *that* particular self-deception.

2. Ok, that's how the poem starts. Now look how it ends, look at its last sentence. What is it saying? Here is poetical license, poetical inversion, gone to perverse extreme. Translation to the rescue and we get: "In labour of the trouble at its fount, Life leads the rebel discords up the sacred mount to an intelligible Lord."

But when we do that we only multiply disturbances precisely because we've played at supplying the poem with an expository form that it doesn't actually have. *Felix culpa*, that game of trying to make sense. Now we see more clearly the problem of that preposition "of," the labour of it (and do we recall—resist the thought!— how we let line 5 go by with its remark about "the language heard of Love"—what's *that* anyhow, what does "of" mean there?).

And dare I ask whether one is permitted to imagine that "rebel" might be taken as a noun and "discords" as a verb?

There is a moral to this text: that we "listen *in* the thought" (not *to* the thought). For thought is here conceived (first) in an analogy with, and (then) as a structure of, musical form and the powerful if fleeting presences of those forms. Should we go that journey, we "may" (should we choose—it *might* happen, and perhaps it will, if we pray for it) begin to think differently ("so may there come"—where would that "there" be? Is "there" an adverb? an expletive?). *Think about it.*

III.

PRINTER'S DEVIL. Ok, let's. Gumbrecht points out that a "'tension'... between presence effects and meaning effects" is the very essence of "the situation of aesthetic experience." He then adds that because these "two dimensions [of the aesthetic situation] will never grow into a stable structure of complimentarity,"

> We must understand that it is not only unnecessary but indeed analytically counterproductive to try and

develop a combination, a complex metaconcept fusing the semiotic and the nonsemiotic definition of signs.

But as Gumbrecht knows, this is exactly what the poets will not, will never, "understand."

FOOTNOTE. Alas, Gumbrecht doesn't get involved with the poets. He hangs around philosophers and critics, whose names are legion in his book: Aristotle and Heidegger way up there, and then a band of contemporary angels: Derrida, Vattimo, Nancy, Bohrer, Butler, Tausssig, Seel. The poets refuse the kinds of understanding these minds covet. And most of all philosophical poets—Dante, Pope, Blake, for instance, and the long line stretching across the nineteenth-century to Meredith. "These two classes of men are always upon earth and they should be enemies. Whoever seeks to reconcile them seeks to destroy existence" (Blake). The "stable structure" that Gumbrecht imagines is, in that context, a nightmare in Aristotelian masquerade.

PRINTER'S DEVIL. The "stable structure," yes, and the analytical "metaconcept" most certainly. But not the "complimentarity," which fairly defines the tension that Gumbrecht values in poetry. It's so *obvious* in Meredith's little sonnet, where the very identity of the words are held in states of tense duplicity: they are at once nouns and verbs, transitive and intransitive, expletives and adverbs, and forms—prepositions, say— that work at several of the many possibilities of meaning those cunning little words are capable of: the OED has more than seven three-column pages devoted to possible meanings for each of the prepositions "in" and "of," and that's only dealing with standard Oxbridge English in Murray's extraordinary late-nineteenth-century snapshot.

FOOTNOTE. And *that's* only to talk about the duplicities at the level of semantics. Or at one level of the semantic matrix. What about deploying a phrase like "primal thunder" for... what exactly? Zeus? Jehovah? Some abstract derivative? Or "rebel discords": how can we not think of the *diabolus in musica* in a poem that has organized itself around forms of dissonance and music. Or the call to Keats in the phrase "the pain of music"—a reference even more oblique but nonetheless unmistakable to a person with a literary lexicon. Here are the unheard melodies forecast by Keats, "The music yearning like a God in pain" ("The Eve of St. Agnes").

PRINTER'S DEVIL. Or the syntaxes that, like the *diabolus in musica*, open many forbidden but interesting doors. "One false note" could be either the subject or the object of the verb "cast." Think about the difference between that choice of syntaxes, and then think what it means to insist on both syntaxes simultaneously.

FOOTNOTE. And beyond those semantic and syntactic duplicities is the very soul (or DNA?) of poetic form—the double helix of its linguistic and prosodic strands promising a composition of expressive patterns that expository prose cannot—would not—dare to attempt. The sonnet is fraught with the promise of its disturbances, all its false notes and rebel discords. The sonnet produces the presence of dynamic order—

immerses us in an experience of that order—even at the elementary line level, for instance here:

> Now seems the language heard of Love as rain
> To make a mire where fruitfulness was meant.

The effect comes from playing the first line's complete syntactic structure against the enjambment revealed with the appearance of the second line. The consequence of that move unsettles all the words. Does "seems" imply deception? What is "the language heard of Love," how do we parse that phrase? Does "heard of" carry the suggestion of hearsay?

PRINTER'S DEVIL. And it's obvious that Gumbrecht is alive to these features of poetical expression: "literary texts have ways of also bringing the presence-dimension of the typography, of the rhythm of the language, and even of the smell of the paper into play." But he resists what he knows. He decides that because linguistic signs are major elements in poetic compositions, "The meaning-dimension will always be dominant when we are reading a [poetic] text." He forgets that in poetry, prosodic elements are as fundamental as linguistic elements. If he had not, his view of musical form might have altered his opinion about the dominations at play in poetical texts: "I believe that the presence-dimension will always dominate when we are listening to music—and at the same time it is true that certain musical structures can evoke certain semantic connotations."

FOOTNOTE. Strange isn't it.

PRINTER'S DEVIL. Not so strange. His own prose is a god yearning in the pain of its meaning dimensions, its residual faith in analytic metaconcepts. It isn't poetry that's the problem, it's our forms of discussion—our commentaries, our analyses, our endless thematizing. We turn poetry into expository prosings.

FOOTNOTE. Sad. Especially when a great philosophical poet—Wordsworth—launched us into reimagining the distinction between poetry and prose. Just look at the expressive consequences, undreamed by Wordsworth. Poets fashioned new ways for installing prose meanings in prosodic forms, and presence-effects in expository conventions.

PRINTER'S DEVIL. For instance? How about a reading list.

FOOTNOTE. If we hadn't thanatized our poetic inheritance so dreadfully...

PRINTER'S DEVIL. Don't you mean *thematized*?

FOOTNOTE. Either way, if we hadn't, the world would be all before us and where to choose a matter of... personal choice. But given where we are—see Gumbrecht—we need some alienation. So for prose meanings in prosodic forms: spend some time with Swinburne, perhaps especially "Anactoria" and "Hertha"; with Meredith ("The Woods of Westermain," or "Earth and Man"), with Hardy (throughout). Presence-effects in expository conventions: Whitman's "Song of Myself"; any moment in Stein's *The Making of Americans*; Stevens's *Notes*; David Jones's *Anathemata*.

IV.

Concluding Unscientific Postscript

"You must go on, I can't go on, I'll go on."

Eunoia: Beauty or Truth (or What?)

Take Home Exam, Final Question (for Extra Credit): "'Eunoia' is the shortest word in English to contain all five vowels, and the word quite literally means 'beautiful thinking." This sentence begins the concluding unscientific postscript to Christian Bök's remarkable book of verse. Discuss Eunoia as an instance of "beautiful thinking."

Skip Thomai: Beware the geeks bearing gifts, Perry. That's a trick question, I'm sure of it—or tricky anyhow.

Perry Calles: Really? How do you know that?

ST: He's always going on in class about how we read things and don't look up the words we don't know the meaning of, right?

PC: Fucking tiresome.

ST: So when I got the question last night I decided to look up that word eunoia and make sure what it means. And guess what. There's no such word in English (or American!). It's not in Murray's OED, it's not in Webster, its not even in Merriam-Webster. What do you think of *that*?!

PC: But it's in Bök's book—it's the epigraph, quoted from that eighteenth-century poem nobody ever read—except maybe Prof the Pedant.

ST: That's the trick. It's "in" that poem *The Triumphs of Temper* by William Hayley but it's only there as a quoted word—and if anybody actually looked at the printed text of the poem they'd see that. It's set off in capital letters—EUNOIA. And Hayley even tells us that it's a word from a different world.

PC: You found a copy of *The Triumphs of Temper*?

ST: Silly boy. It's on the internet, like everything else. And I did more than that. I went and found where the word comes from. It's Greek. And it doesn't mean "beautiful thinking" at all—as we'd have known if Bök had just quoted the next line of the passage he gives as his epigraph: "Benevolence the name she bears on earth." Look it up in any Greek dictionary. It means "kindness" or "good will."

PC: But if Hayley quotes the word and Bök lifts it over into his poem, then it's "in English," right? And if

Hayley's poem translates EUVOIA first into EUNOIA and then into Benevolence in his poem, why shouldn't Bök translate it to Beautiful Thinking? Especially since he specifies that it means what it means "quite literally." Bök's book only works "quite literally."

ST: Right—and that's the tricky part. EUVOIA first gets to be "the shortest word in English with all five vowels" when it's published in 1780 in *The Triumphs of Temper* under the signs EUNOIA and Benevolence. Then it just starts spreading like a virus through printing after printing of Hayley's poem—there were at least fourteen separate editions published by 1817, and that's only counting the ones issued by the official publisher, Cadell! But through all that the word is only *in* English formally and bibliographically. Not literally, not yet.

PC: Cool. It gets in literally with *Eunoia* where Bök gives it its literal meaning, Beautiful Thinking. In Hayley it gets to mean EUNOIA and Benevolence. Before that it's just, well, EUVOIA. And now Bök's made everybody think it means what he says it means.

ST: Exactly—and presto, Bök starts a new literary movement, "The New Ennui," announced in what the professor calls Bök's "concluding unscientific postscript."

PC: Not so new. It's just a new name for an old set of tricks. Call it the Humpty Dumpty School.

> "When I use a word," Humpty Dumpty said, in rather a scornful tone, "it means just what I choose it to mean—neither more nor less."

> "The question is," said Alice, "whether you can make words mean so many different things."
>
> "The question is," said Humpty Dumpty, "which is to be master—that's all."

ST: Interesting. That makes me think Bök went to a different school altogether. Humpty's school has a headmaster who talks like God Almighty—one of those old types my dad told me about. I think they're mostly dead now. But the New Ennui is poetry without a personality. It's beyond even O'Hara's Personism. It's pure X-Gen.

PC: *Im*pure I'd say. About as far from a Slacker mode as possible: "a Sisyphusaean spectacle of its labour" that "required seven years of daily perseverance for its consummation" (*Eunoia*). That's a "New Ennui" alright—grandstanding in Bök's signature flatland wit. Ennui sending out its coded message: "un oui."

ST: And there's more there there than meets the ear. "*Its* labour," "*its* consummation." This isn't Jacob laboring for Rachel to beget all the legitimate children of Israel. It isn't even Jacob with *all* those wives of his, and all those multiplying offspring he was told to spread around, legitimate and illegitimate. Jacob's story isn't part of this story at all. *Eunoia* is poetry as parthogenesis, with Christian Bök as midwife or voyeur...

PC: Or star-gazing shepherd?

ST: Whatever... and *Eunoia* as Molly Bloom text-messaging to her lovers, her readers: "And yes I said yes

I will Yes." "A paradise of pleasure and ennui," as another poet of the same kind once wrote.

And it's not as if Bök hasn't told us what *Eunoia*'s about, at least in his view. There's 'Pataphysics out of Alfred Jarry and OULIPO, and then there's 'Pataphysics out of bpnichol, Steve McCaffery, Christopher Dewdney and their various "imaginary academies": the Toronto Research Group, the Institute for Linguistic Ontogenetics, The 'Pataphysical Hardware Company. Bök's Canadian 'Pataphysicians are come to evacuate the illusions of place, time and meaning that were established by

> the environmental mythopoiesis of... [Northrop] Frye, [Margaret] Atwood, and [Robert] Kroetsch (for whom literature is merely the side effect of a geography—the surreal terrain of a collective unconscious... Canadian 'Pataphysics opposes such mysticism, treating literature not as a mythopoeic, but as a cyborganic phenomenon.

PC: Huh?

ST: That's really saying something, isn't it!

PC: If you say so.

ST: I don't say so, Bök does in his book *'Pataphysics. The Poetics of an Imaginary Science*, which "reflects the influence of Jarry on my own poetic career." Bök writes a narrative of the historical emergence of his work, tracing out his view of procedural writing and the "potential literature" displayed in *Chrystallography* and *Eunoia*. "To be literary," he says in *'Pataphysics*, "is to pose imaginary solutions to problematic formulations." The problematic formulations are the set of arbitrary rules, or constraints, that are established before any text actually unfolds. The constraints are laid down as a kind of scientific hypothesis that, when actually tested out, reveals what Blake called "the infinite which was hid" in the apparently determinate surfaces of things. Not *beneath* the surfaces, as a symbolist or a surrealist view would argue, but within and as the surfaces themselves, which have no meaning beyond themselves. They're autopoietic phenomena, whose "growth [has] no guerdon / But only to grow," as Swinburne argued in his poetic manifesto for a similar view of poetic forms ("Hertha"). Taking his cue from Hans Vaihinger, Bök calls this an as *if* writing—a ludic exploration of the "combinatoric potentialities" of alphabetic signs. "The truth of the ludic abides by no belief; instead, such truth is *entertained* as one of many hypothetical alternatives. It is merely a potentiality" (*'Pataphysics* again).

PC: So Bök's *'Pataphysics. The Poetics of an Imaginary Science* is like Poe's "The Philosophy of Composition." Poe tells us how to go about writing poetry by telling us how he went about writing "The Raven." And Bök's study of 'pataphysical poetics is his critical explanation of *Eunoia*'s "Beautiful Thinking." Is that right?

ST: Well Bök goes into much greater depth but, essentially, yes—they're the same kind of critical work. And now that you mention it, they have a lot more in common than a shared genre. They're both manifestoes for self-conscious procedural writing. "Most writers," Poe impishly says, "poets in especial—prefer having it understood that they compose by a species of fine frenzy—an ecstatic intuition." Not Poe. On the contrary, his essay lays out "step by step, the processes by which... one of his compositions attained its ultimate point of completion" (Poe, "The Philosophy of Composition"). Note that "*Its* completion"! And remember "The New Ennui": "*its* labour," "*its* consummation"! Poe is writing what Bök calls "lucid writing" about a poetics of lucid writing, which "does not concern itself with the transparent transmission of a message... [but] with the exploratory examination of its own pattern." For both Poe and Bök, "What is at stake is the status of poetry in a world of science."

PC: True. But not true enough. Bök's "survey" of procedural writing continually stresses its "ludic" character. And that description would rhyme well with Poe's outrageously witty essay except for one thing: Bök's book, unlike Poe's essay, is about as far from a ludic performance as one could imagine. Look at this passage, for instance—and it's entirely characteristic.

> Imaginary academies such as these all imply that the mythic desire for cultural essences can only reinforce the metaphysical theorization of an imperial paradigm.... All theories in effect subordinate thought to the nomic instrumentation of a royal science, whereas research coordinates thought through the ludic experimentalism of a nomad science. For the research of such imaginary academies, language itself represents a cyborganic phenomenon, in which every text becomes a poetic device, a novel brand of "book-machine," whose virologic mechanism uses us more than we use it.
>
> —'Pataphysics

Now if that particular text had become a poetic device we'd have no problem with it. The high-falutin parallel of "the nomic instrumentation of a royal science" (bad, bad!) with "the ludic experimentalism of a nomad science" (Look! We have come through!) isn't ludic, it's pretentious—ludicrous. *Un*beautiful thinking. How it ever turned into *Eunoia* is a miracle of rare device.

ST: Does ludic writing in this mode have to be funny?

PC: No, but it does have to be *lucid* in Bök's (and Poe's) special sense: it has to make a literal demonstration of its argument. Beautiful thinking has to be thinking realized at the aesthetic level—thinking as an artifice of style and formal procedures. That would be what *Eunoia* does and what Bök's critical book—quite unlike Poe's essay—doesn't do. And *Eunoia* does it throughout the book—even in the witty preface that comes into the book as a postscript, like Walter Scott's last chapter to his great experimental fiction *Waverley*.

    So you're right to point out Bök's sly use of the pronoun "it" in "The New Ennui." That's what I call ludic and lucid. Or look how he plays with the convention of an "Acknowledgments": "Special thanks to Darren Weschler-Henry (who drove the car while I read Perec), and special thanks to Natalie Caple (who let me work while she slept)". There they are, what every poet needs: a poetic guide and attendant spirit, on one hand, and the Muse on the other. Darren Weschler-Henry as Virgil, with (just perhaps) a side glance at the car in Cocteau's *Orphée*; and Natalie Caple as Sleeping Beauty, a Blessed Damozel in oneiric touch with the regions of imaginative potential being implemented by the super-conscious and determined poet.

ST: Beautiful thoughts! You'll be writing them up for that extra-credit exam question I suppose.

PC: What else? We want to be practical about this beauty thing, right? So to answer the question we'll show how *Eunoia* argues that *there are no ideas but in beautiful things*. Tell me that idea won't score with Herr Professor!

ST: Which means we'll have to show how it constructs its arguments not logically but aesthetically. "Quite literally."

PC: Quite.

ST: So why not start by reading the bibliographical object published by Coach House Press—that *ding an sich*? Like the different verses in the book, *it* has a voice (as it were) too. Its cover is a speaking image and so is its frontispiece, but they address us in nonalphabetic languages. The book then comes to our aid, explaining the visible language of those premonitions:

> COVER IMAGE. "Of Yellow" is a polychromatic transcription of the sonnet "Voyelle" by Arthur Rimbaud. Vowels have been replaced with blocks of colour according to the schema described in the sonnet itself: "*A noir, E blanc, I rouge, U vert, O bleu: voyelles.*" All other letters, commas, and spaces are grey....

> FRONTISPIECE. "Vowels Swivel" is a nested set
> of transparent geometric solids (each one gener-
> ated by rotating a given vowel around a vertical
> axis: A (cone); E (cylinder); I (line); O (sphere);
> U (paraboloid).
>
> —*Eunoia*

The title page identifies Bök as the "author" of the
book's verses, but who has authored this text? Or who
is the agent responsible for the cover and frontispiece?
Anonymous? Not at all. *It* is. The book speaks for itself.

PC: So it does, and in more ways than your quotation
meets the mind. Here's how it *actually*—"quite literally"—meets the eye reading the book:

> COVER IMAGE. "Of Yellow" is a polychromatic tran-
> scription of the sonnet "Voyelle" by Arthur Rimbaud.
> Vowels have been replaced with blocks of colour
> according to the schema described in the sonnet itself:
> "*A noir, E blanc, I rouge, U vert, O bleu: voyelles.*" All
> other letters, commas, and spaces are grey. The image
> has appeared on the cover of *Sulfur* 44 (Spring 1999).

> FRONTISPIECE. "Vowels Swivel" is a nested set of trans-
> parent geometric solids (each one generated by rotat-
> ing a given vowel around a vertical axis: A (cone);
> E (cylinder); I (line); O (sphere); U (paraboloid).

And that layout is important—as deliberate as Poe's
ideas about a philosophical poetic method. Because it
rhymes exactly with the deliberated layout of the
book's other prose-poetic texts: "Eunoia," "Emended
Excess," and "The New Ennui." These too are left and
right justified into blocks of text, with the units of

"Eunoia" and "Emended Excess" having the additional constraint of a set number of lines for each integral unit, with one unit printed on each page. "Emended Excess" is laid out in blocks of eleven lines while the individual letter sections of "Eunoia" have, respectively, twelve (A), eleven (E), eleven (I), thirteen (O), and twelve (U) lines. So the first unit of "Chapter E" begins:

> Enfettered, these sentences repress free speech. The text deletes selected letters. We see the revered exegete reject metred verse: the sestet, the tercet—even *les scènes élevées en grec*. He rebels. He sets new precedents. He lets cleverness exceed decent levels. He eschews the esteemed genres, the expected themes—even *les belles lettres en vers*. He prefers the perverse French esthetes:

and so forth. And note how the procedural rule leads this literal being to assume a kind of life of its own. "The text," we learn, is itself an agent of its own evolving self. And "the revered exegete"? Is this another name for "The text" acting as its own procedural interpreter? And that "We,"—who is that? The reader? Other textual agents who are observing the action as it unfolds? Or the "He"? That surely *is* "The text" repressing free, spontaneous speech, deleting letters, rejecting metred verse and taking sides with those perverse aesthetic frogs.

ST: "The book speaks for itself." That's good. And it does because it "moans round with many voices," nearly all of them *not* Christian Bök's. He speaks *in propria persona* only in "The New Ennui," and even there he appears as only one agent in a much larger textual event and experience. Hassan Abd Al-Hassad, the central character in Section A of "Eunoia," is in certain obvious ways an even more prominent agent.

PC: A poetical character from a recognizable gene pool: Childe Harold or Sordello or Prufrock or Berryman's Henry or the implicit human agents in Hejinian's *My Life* or Howe's *Pythagorean Silence*. Or Jarry's Ubu.

ST: Well yes, but a more specific sub-type. And Ubu's relation to Section U shows the difference. The Ubu character there is a derivative function of Jarry's Ubu—not at all the latter, but what the latter might become. He is a heretofore unrealized set of Ubuist possibilities—if Ubu were constrained to become even less human, even more literal, than Jarry's Ubu. So even Jarry's Ubu—or Djuna Barnes's Ryder—are too human. Hassan's closest relatives would be Stevens's Crispin or the Chieftan Iffucan of Azcan or the Queen in Laura Riding's poetic tales.

PC: Or Serena in Hayley's *The Triumphs of Temper*!

ST: Right. But again the comparisons fall short. Like the Ubu of Section U, Hassan is a name that turns from a name to a word, and having made that turn it turns to other words (in another sense) to discover its secret lives: "Hassan can start a war"; "Hassan can watch aghast as databanks at NASDAQ graph hard data and chart a NASDAQ crash." Hassan can grab, want, watch, rant, talk, canvass, and gag. He has lots of capabilities. He also actually *does* things: "Hassan balks at all sacral tasks" and "drafts a Magna Charta." And while we might have learned that he could clasp, jab, grab, pack, stand, and stalk—among other things—here Hassan doesn't, though all of these acts and many more come to pass in his orbit. If Hassan is a purely potential figure, he's quite specific—indeed, unique—in eunoian actuality. A world lies before him, where to *choose*.

PC: But of course Hassan doesn't do the choosing. Christian Bök does.

ST: But of course. But then who is Christian, what is he, that heaven itself commends him here through the sublime court of *The Triumphs of Temper*? In Section O, the key generating word is "who," as "can" is the key word in Section A (and as sub-semantic guttural forms generate Section U). So "who" is the form assumed by the deliberating Christian Bök in Section O, and who rapidly metastasizes into profs, dons, monks, God, blond trollops and blond showfolk, snobs, Moors from Morocco, cooks, crooks, Goths, and so forth. Christian Bök becomes barely a face in the Hugolian crowd, a kind of disappearing Baudelairean god. *Eunoia* is a critical reflection on the idea of identity—and a revelation of what Blake called "The will of the Immortal" that has always existed, before there were any gods, and after they have gone:

> Earth was not: nor globes of attraction
> The will of the Immortal expanded
> Or contracted his all flexible senses.
> Death was not, but eternal life sprung.
> —*The Book of Urizen*

PC: An extremely beautiful thought.

ST: I'm thinking Prof will think so too. He's a flaming anti-theist!

PC: He's also as perverse as those "French esthetes" in Section E. So we really have to nail this argument down. And Section I is the way to go! It begins in an aggressive first person:

> Writing is inhibiting. Sighing, I sit, scribbling in ink this pidgin script. I sing with nihilistic witticism, disciplining signs with trifling gimmicks—impish hijinks which highlight stick sigils. Isn't it glib? Isn't it chic? I fit childish insights within rigid limits, writing shtick which might instill priggish misgivings in critics blind with hindsight. I dismiss nit-picking criticism which flirts with philistinism. I bitch; I kibitz—griping whilst criticizing dimwits, sniping whilst indicting nitwits, dismissing simplistic thinking, in which phillipic wit is still illicit.

But this first person is an impish hijink, though we don't perhaps see that right away. I soldiers on through the unfolding stanzas: "I pitch in, fixing things. I rig this / winch with its wiring"; "Hiking in British districts, I hike"; "Fishing till twilight, I sit, drifting in this birch skiff." But as we read we wonder about the what and where and who of this stick sigil: "Which / blind spirit is whining in this whistling din?" Is it a "blind witch... midwifing its misbirth"? These beautiful questions we might have posed ourselves! But I is there before us, leading us on. "Is it this / thin, sickish girl [and who would that be? The blind witch?], twitching in fits, whilst writing / things in spirit-writing? If it isn't—it is I; it is I..." And through it all our old friend it is back suggesting—yikes!—that "it is I."

But the piece of resistance is saved for the end, I's last stand:

> Thinking within strict limits is stifling. Whilst Viking Knights fight griffins, I skirmish with this riddling Sphinx (this sigil—I). I print lists, filing things (kin with kin, ilk with ilk), inscribing this distinct sign, listing things in which its imprint is intrinsic. I find its missing links, divining its implicit tricks. I find it whilst skin-diving in Fiji; I find it whilst picknicking in Linz. I find it in Inniskillin; I find it in Mississippi. I find it whilst skiing in Minsk. (Is this intimism civilizing if Klimpt limns it, if Liszt lilts it?) I sigh, I lisp. I finish writing this writ, signing it, kind sir: NIHIL DICIT, FINI.

The opening sentences recall nothing so much as Borges' essay (or is it a story?), "Borges and I": "I skirmish with this riddling / Sphinx (this sigil—I)."

ST: Or Hollander's *Reflections on Espionage*? Or some of Merrill's early poems—like "Mirror" or "Charles on Fire."

PC: Sure. Beautiful thinking is often a world of mirrors and codes. Here it is Nothing that speaks, a first person (major man!) we can watch disappearing in the case ending of another language. Most beautiful of all, we can watch it appearing as well, and at the same time, in the poetic form summoned at this end of Section I: that special kind of "riddling Sphinx" known as the Enigma. "I find it whilst skin-diving in Fiji; I find it whilst picknicking in Linz. I find it in Inniskillin; I find it in Mississippi. I find it whilst skiing in Minsk." Another "Enigma on the Letter I," mirroring—recollecting—those (once) famous lines of

Catherine Fanshawe:

> I am not in youth, nor in manhood or age,
>   But in infancy ever am known.
> I'm a stranger alike to the fool and the sage,
> And though I'm distinguished on history's page,
>   I always am greatest alone.
>
> I'm not in the earth, nor the sun, nor the moon;
>   You may search all the sky, I'm not there;
> In the morning and evening, though not in the noon,
> You may plainly perceive me, for, like a balloon,
>   I am always suspended in air.
>
> Though disease may possess me, and sickness, and pain,
>   I am never in sorrow or gloom.
> Though in wit and in wisdom I equally reign,
> I'm the heart of all sin, and have long lived in vain,
>   Yet I ne'er shall be found in the tomb.

The comic will of the Immortal—that eternal life should spring. It's a beautiful way of thinking, and "Benevolence [is] the name she bears on earth."

ST: But of course it *is* only all autopoietic. I think of Tennyson, who published a very similar book in 1830 called *Poems, Chiefly Lyrical*. His friend Arthur Hallam then wrote a brilliant study of that book and its "poetry of sensation." His main point was that Tennyson's verse created a drama of a mind thinking through images and prosody. Another friend, Richard Trench, read it the same way but while Hallam was wild with no regret at what Tennyson was doing, Trench came to a rather different conclusion: "Tennyson," he said, "we cannot live in art."

PC: We're not talking about living, we're talking about thinking.

ST: But Trench's idea is that if the thinking in the poem is only a literal or aesthetic drama, what will we have except the shop-talk of a Bohemian or an Uptown Grub Street?

ST: Do poems think? I don't *think* so! They're like computers—prosthetic devices. They're magic mirrors we hold up to help us think more clearly about things that matter.

PC: Like the wrath of Achilles say? Section E of *Eunoia* parodies the *Iliad*, thinking about it not as the narrative of a brutal, heroic society, but as a certain set of deployable signs.

ST: A travesty.

PC: Lewis Carroll and Edward Lear triumph in their travesties. So does Byron, so does Shakespeare. Give me a fucking *break*!

ST: Fair enough. Besides, it's not as if *Eunoia* doesn't include itself in its art of sinking. Or us. "Isn't it glib? Isn't it chic?" I suppose I'm one of those "critics blind with hindsight"—who *didn't* take courses from the Yale School these past 50 years?! And then there's... who? I? It? Hassan? Somebody anyhow—why not the cyborganic (posthuman?) Christian Bök, working away to "fit childish insights within rigid limits, writing shtick."

PC: "Childish insights"!! The gloss on that would be the Christian's: "Unless you become again as little children you shall not enter the kingdom of heaven." So here we have a whole new set of Christian games. And "shtick" tells us what kind they are: "shtick," Yiddish from the German Stück, meaning "piece." This Bökian book is *all* of a piece because it communicates in pieces, forcing us to look away from words as referential signs and consider them as physical things made up of pieces and parts that can be shifted about and re-arranged. The block formalities of the stanzas of "Eunoia" inflect the work arithmetically and geometrically. We count the lines per unit and the units per section because we *have* to if we're to read it. But when we've done that we aren't delivered over to a hermeneutic "meaning," we simply see the work and its parts more clearly. Or look at—*look* at!—the poem "Vowels."

    loveless vessels

    we vow
    solo love

    we see
    love solve loss

    else we see
    love sow woe

    selves we woo
    we lose

    losses we levee
    we owe

we sell
loose vows

so we love
less well

so low
so level

wolves evolve

The anonymous explicator of the Cover Image points out how Rimbaud's thought about the expressive equivalence of vowels and colors can be, has been, realized. And then the book's frontispiece carries the idea further, showing that they (might) have geometric shapes too. And then comes this anagrammaton "Vowels," breaking "every letter in the title" into pieces to produce ten new permutations. Each of these emerge as distinct piecemeal units.

ST: But the real piece of insistence here is this larger coherent thing, this poem, which unfolds as another piece of language now arranging itself, as if by some Brownian poetic law, at a different scale. The poem is "quite literally" a Mandelbrot set. And wildly wonderful as "Vowels" is, look at the text titled "W." Talk about "childish games"!

It is the V you double, not the U, as if to use
two valleys in a valise is to savvy the vacuum
of a vowel at a powwow in between sawteeth.

You have to read this with your eyes and ears. "V you double" begins the game, putting out a signal we must read as three letters, the V, the U, and the double-U made by doubling the V. And this letter, this W, is a form of two U's to be used (for instance) as if one imagined a valise with two slots (a W form) as two valleys—and to make that imagining in order to gain some procedural opportunities. You (U) might double the form as "valleys" and "valise," or you might see "the vacuum of a vowel" in any carefully observed W, an absent vowel imaginable between the W's two v forms, a vowel imaginably gone because—as when two W's get together to powwow—the letter's *saw*teeth can be *seen*.

Then each stanza of the text develops various permutations being imagined for the letter W. The last is particularly delicious:

> It is the name for an X whose V does not view
> the surface of a lake but the mirror on a wall,
> where U & you become a tautonym, a continuum.

There's a riddle to be solved: "When is W "the name for an X"? Answer: W is the name for an X when we don't see the letter as two v's standing atop each other—that letter would be, as it were, a reflection of a v on the shore of a lake—but as a letter formed of two adjacent v's, each a mirror image of the other. And *see*ing that, *think* of the implications! In this letterspace we glimpse the possibility of an indefinitely extensive system of interchangeable signs. "U & you" become equivalent, each a figure of the other and signaled as such by the visible figure—the sign—of their equivalence: not the word "and" but the sign of that word, the ampersand. In aesthetic thinking like that, to encounter a word like "continuum" is to be able to see in its literal form a sign that we *are* the forms by which we try to reflect on ourselves and know who we are.

PC: Kick-Ass, man. If that's not an A I'm not an anthromorph.

Prescriptions

Certain cultures never yield to force,
Care won't do, nor will, not even virtue.
One needs patience hunting down a source.

To take a journey, start with few provisions,
In this place every stranger is a guest.
Expect nothing when you make decisions.

The rites of passage disallow prevention,
Here are gods who do not brook demands:
Only grace gives meaning to intention.

Also available from Prickly Paradigm Press:

continued